TALKIN' SOCCER

BY James Buckley Jr. • ILLUSTRATED BY James Horvath

The Child's World®
childsworld.com

Published by The Child's World®
1980 Lookout Drive • Mankato, MN 56003-1705
800-599-READ • www.childsworld.com

Photos: Cover: Sergey Nivens/Shutterstock.
Interior: AP Photos: 4; François Mori 14.
Dreamstime.com: Salajean 10. Newscom: Randy Litzinger/Icon SW 5; Frank Hoermann/Sven Simon/Picture Alliance 18; Ken Levine/Icon SMI 20.
Shutterstock: Robo Michalec 1; Ververidis Vasilis 6T; Gresei 6B; halfpoint 7; Vasyl Shuga 8; LifeStyle Graphic 9; CLS Digital Arts 11; ljansempoi 12; Laszlo Szirtesi 13; Wavebreakmedia 15; thanhtrong007 16; Dzuirek 17; maxisport 19.

Copyright © 2020 by The Child's World®
All rights reserved. No part of this book may be reproduced or utilized in any form or by any means without written permission from the publisher.

ISBN 9781503835733
LCCN 2019943131

Printed in the United States of America

TABLE OF CONTENTS

Introduction . . . 4
Gear Up . . . 6
On the Field . . . 8
Playing the Game . . . 10
Stat City . . . 14
Soccer People . . . 16
Fun Stuff . . . 18
More Slang . . . 20

Glossary . . . 22
Find Out More . . . 23
Index and About the Author . . . 24

INTRODUCTION

Name the Game: Soccer or Football?

Most of the world calls this sport "football." That makes sense. You kick the ball with your foot! The United States, Canada, and a few other places call it soccer. That name comes from "association football." The sport was called that in the late 1800s. In America, that was shortened to "assoc." And that became . . . *soccer*!

Welcome! Before you kick me around, find out how to "talk soccer" inside!

One-Name Wonders

Many soccer stars are so famous, they are known by just one name.

Pelé (Edson Arantes do Nascimento)

Messi (Lionel Messi)

Ronaldo (Cristiano Ronaldo)

Mia (Mia Hamm)

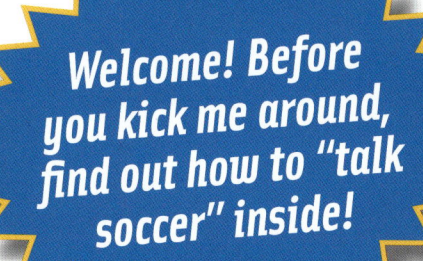

I scored more than 1,200 goals for Brazil and for my pro teams!

Alphabet Soup

Many groups help put on soccer games around the world. Here are some of the biggest.

FIFA: Federation Internationale de Football Association, which organizes the World Cup tournaments

MLS: Major League Soccer, the American/Canadian pro league for men

NWSL: National Women's Soccer League, the pro league for women

UEFA: Union of European Football Associations, which organizes club soccer in Europe

▲ *Pelé was a superstar in the 1950s, 1960s, and 1970s. He played forward. He thrilled fans with amazing skills and joy for the game.*

Gear Up

You don't need much gear to play soccer. Players wear a jersey and shorts. Most wear long socks. Team clothing in soccer is called "kit." Many famous teams have very colorful kit. The only pads most players use cover their shins.

▲ Superstar Lionel Messi shows off the kit he wears when he plays for Barcelona in Spain.

The Ball

Soccer balls come in different sizes. The pros use a No. 5. Younger players might use a No. 4 or a No. 3. The No. 5 is 8.6 inches (22 cm) across. The most famous soccer ball style is black-and-white. This kind has 12 **pentagons** and 20 **hexagons**. Newer styles have wild patterns and different numbers of panels.

The Shoes

Players wear leather shoes. Call them boots or kicks! The shoe bottoms are made of hard plastic or rubber. Cleats or "studs" stick out from the bottom. These help players run well on grass and dirt.

▲ Soccer shoes come in a ton of different colors and styles.

Don't worry! It doesn't hurt when players kick me with their soccer shoes!

The Goalie Gloves

Only one player can touch the ball with her hands. Goalkeepers ("goalies" or "keepers") wear padded gloves. This helps them stop super-fast or high-flying shots.

ON THE FIELD

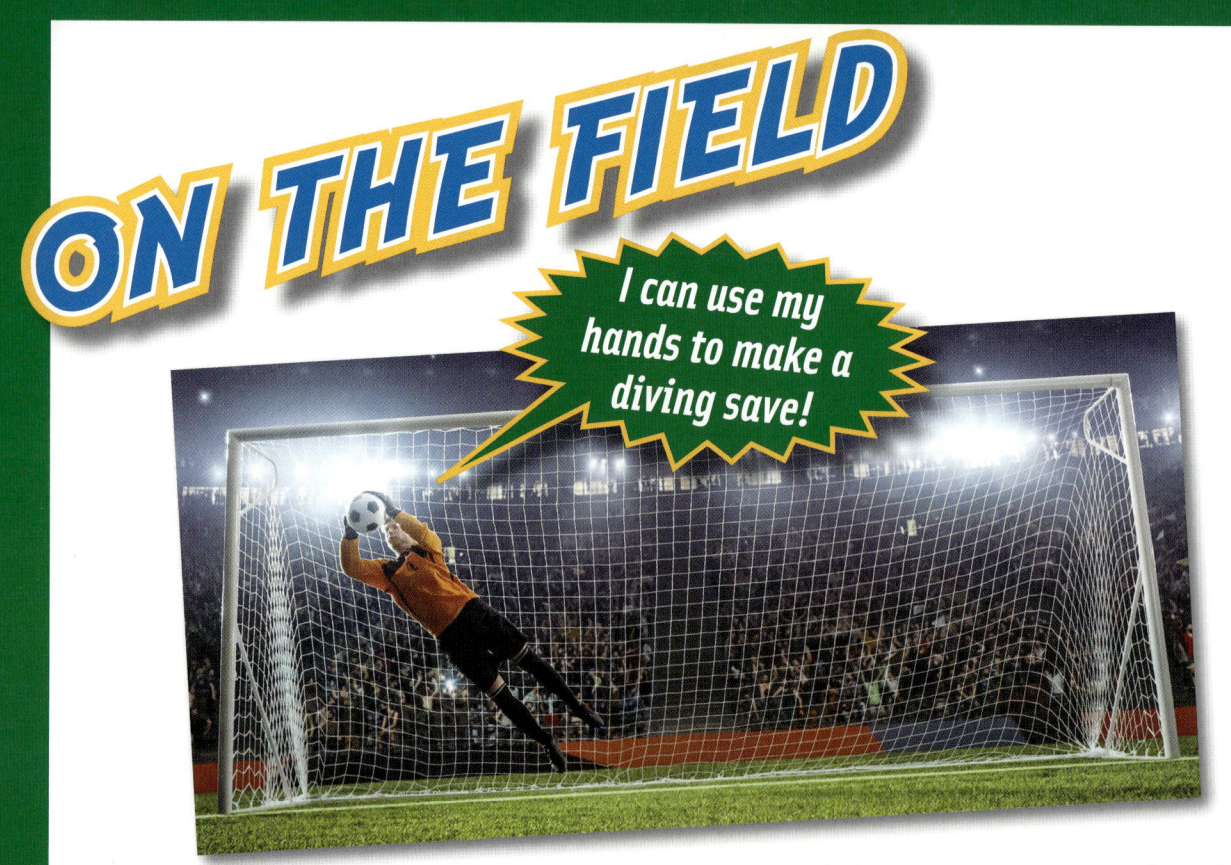

I can use my hands to make a diving save!

▲ *A soccer goal is 8 yards (7.3 m) across. It is 8 feet (2.4 m) high.*

The Field

Soccer fields are huge! A whole American football field can fit into a pro soccer field . . . with room to spare! At each end are end lines. Sidelines mark the edges of the field. Lines painted on the field show the center and the penalty area. (See picture at right.) Want to sound like a soccer pro? Call a soccer field "the pitch."

Indoor Soccer

Futsal is a form of soccer played indoors. Five players on each team kick around a smaller ball. The field is about as big as a hockey rink or a basketball court. Futsal is very fast-moving. Players make amazing dribbling moves!

8

6, 10, and 18

Here are three numbers in a book about words! On each end of a soccer field are two large boxes. The larger is 18 yards (16.5 m) deep. This is the penalty area. Inside this is the goalie box, which is six yards (5.5 m) deep. The "penalty spot" is painted 10 yards (9.1 m) from the goal line. When a penalty kick is awarded, it is taken from that spot.

The center circle

A 10-yard (9.1-m) circle is painted at midfield. The game starts from the center of the circle. A game starts over after a goal from that point, too.

Sidelines

If the ball passes over these lines, it is out of bounds. You can also say "into touch."

Playing the Game

Soccer is sometimes called "the beautiful game." Players move the ball around the field by kicking it. As they move and run, they are graceful and powerful. Their skills with the ball are what fans think are beautiful.

▲ *Players use their body to block the defense. They control the ball by dribbling it with their feet.*

Dribbling

Players run with the ball near their feet by dribbling. This means making small taps and touches on the ball to keep it moving. Great dribblers can use every part of their feet. They are able to dribble right past or between defenders using tricky moves.

Passing

A pass moves the ball from one player to the other. A pass can roll on the ground or fly through the air. A good pass lands right where a teammate can reach it. A bad pass goes to the other team!

Goooooalll! Soccer players love to celebrate when they score!

Shooting

Take the shot! That means to kick the ball toward the goal. Most shots are kicked. Others can be made by bouncing the ball off the head. Players can even shoot with the knees, shins, or chest! If the shot goes in the goal, it's time for a celebration!

▲ *A great soccer shot is hit with the top of the foot. Aim for the ball with the laces on your boot!*

If I do this right, it won't hurt. I can help my team with a pass or a shot.

Heading

Young players should not hit the ball with their head. Older players learn the correct way to do this. Players knock the ball with their *forehead*. Heading the ball is a good way to clear the ball away from your goal. Some players can shoot the ball at the goal using their heads.

◄ *When heading, this player will move his body to the ball, not whip his neck.*

Defending

A defender in soccer "marks" an opponent. That means she stands or runs near another player. She tries to kick the ball away or even steal it. Teams work together on defense to make sure all opponents are marked.

Playing Goalie

Goalies prevent shots from going in the goal. They dive, leap, and slide to stop the ball. They can use their hands, so they try to catch the ball. If they can't, they push or punch it away from the goal.

Tackle!

Expert players can make a slide tackle. This means sliding on the ground with one foot forward. That foot knocks the ball away from an opponent. Be careful! If you miss the ball, you can be called for a foul.

A goalie's life is 88 minutes of boredom and two minutes of fear!

◄ *A perfect tackle! The player in blue slides her foot into the ball to knock it away.*

STAT CITY

We helped the United States win the 2019 Women's World Cup!

Soccer doesn't have as many stats as other sports do. Still, numbers are important in soccer. Keep track of your favorites with these key digits.

▶ *American stars Mallory Pugh and Megan Rapinoe show how they celebrate a goal!*

Count 'em Up

Players on offense pile up a few key stats. They keep track of how many shots they take. They also count how many are "on target." That is, shots that went in, or would have if the goalie didn't stop them. Players earn **assists** for making a pass that leads to a goal. And, of course, the most important stat is how many goals are scored!

Great save! Goalies have to learn to dive to block shots.

Goals-Against

You can see how good a goalie is by his goals-against average (GAA). Take the number of goals he has let in. Divide that by the number of games he has played. The result is the GAA. Most great goalies have a GAA less than 2.0!

A Clean Sheet

Is this about laundry? No, a clean sheet is when a goalie does not allow a goal. It means the scoring sheet is clean (or empty) against the goalie's team. It's also called a shutout.

SOCCER PEOPLE

Players, coaches, referees, and fans all pack into the soccer stadium for every game. Let's meet them.

For rough fouls, I can show a player a yellow card. That means "be careful"! Two yellow cards and the player is kicked out! I can also show a red card for a very bad foul. That sends a player right off the field!

The Whistlers

The referee ("ref") is the person in the middle. The ref runs up and down the field with the players. If he sees a foul, he blows a whistle to stop play. Fouls turn into free kicks for the team that was fouled. On each sideline, an assistant referee helps. He shows which team has knocked a ball out of play. He also calls offside.

Defenders

A line of defenders plays in front of the goalie. They try to stop the other team from shooting. Defenders are sometimes called fullbacks.

Goalkeeper

Call her the keeper or the goalie. Inside the penalty area, she is in charge. She grabs any ball she can reach. Then she throws or kicks the ball to a teammate. She also knocks away any shot that she can.

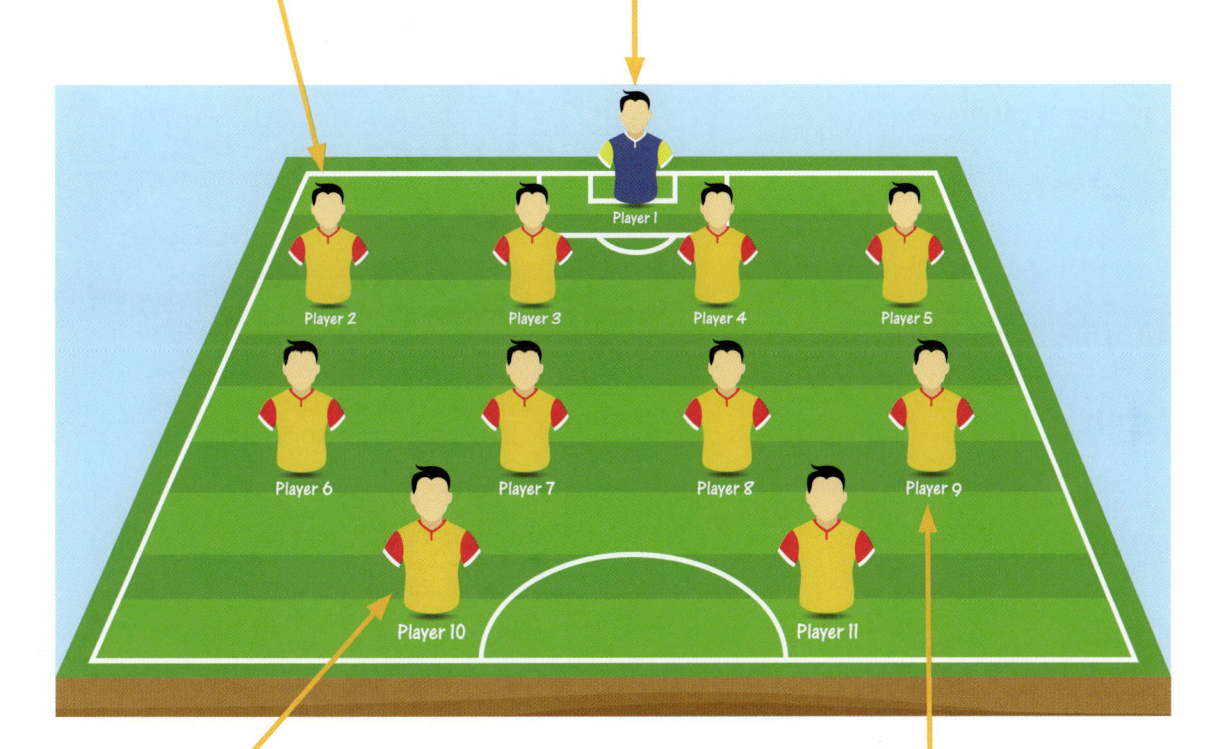

Forwards

These are the players on offense closest to the enemy goal. They look for passes that they can shoot toward the goal. The top scorers are called "strikers."

Midfielders

Behind the forwards is a group of all-around players. Midfielders, or halfbacks, play both offense and defense. They run the most of any position. They need to be good dribblers and passers.

FUN STUFF

Here are some other words and terms you'll hear around the soccer pitch.

Chip
A short pass or shot hit in the air straight ahead of the passer.

Clear
To kick or head the ball away from your own goal area.

Cross
A pass kicked across the front of the goal.

Extra time
Referees are in charge of the game time, usually 90 minutes. They can add extra to make up for time lost for injuries or other events.

▲ *This wall of players leaps to block a free kick from reaching the goal behind them.*

Soccer is the most popular sport in the world. Here is what the game is called in some big soccer-loving countries.

Futbol	Mexico, Spain, Argentina, etc.
Calcio	Italy
Fussball	Germany
Football	England
Zuqiu	China

18

Free kick
A kick given after a foul.

Near post
The goal post closest to where the ball is on the field.

Offside
A foul called when a player is beyond the final defender when the ball is passed toward her.

Set piece
Any free kick, including corner kicks.

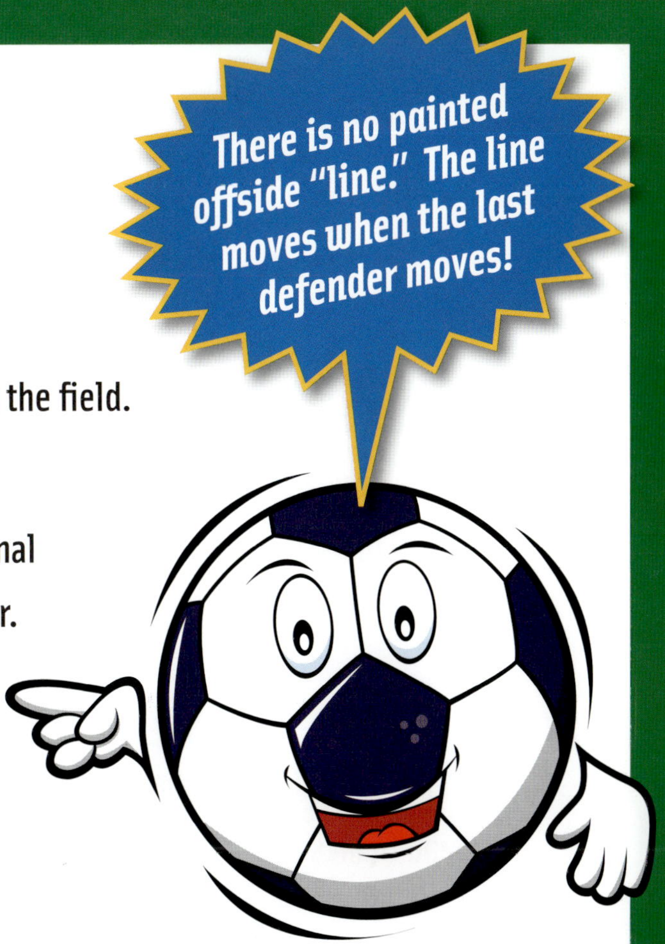

There is no painted offside "line." The line moves when the last defender moves!

▼ *Players must use both hands from over their head on a throw-in.*

Switch fields
Kick the ball from one side of the field to the opposite side.

Throw in
The way to put the ball back into play after it goes out on either side of the field.

Wall
A line of defenders who can stand 10 yards in front of a free kick.

More Slang

People have been kicking round balls around for hundreds of years. It might even be thousands of years! Today's players and fans are still coming up with new ways to talk about their game. Here are a few of our favorites.

Watch for juggling into a bicycle kick that turns into a golazo!

Bicycle kick
When a player kicks his foot high above his head to kick the ball backward

Dummy
When a player steps over a pass to let a teammate behind her get the ball

Flick
A pass or shot made with a quick, small movement of the foot

Golazo
A really terrific goal

▶ Players shooting with a bicycle kick can't see the goal behind them!

Into touch
The soccer term for when a ball goes out of bounds

Juggling
The act of keeping a ball in the air using feet and other body parts

Nutmeg
To pass or shoot the ball between a defender's feet

PK
Stands for "penalty kick." (However, soccer people never say "DK" for direct kick or "FK" for free kick! Only the penalty kick is known by its initials.)

Punt
A long, high kick made by the goalie to move the ball down the field

Upper V
Nickname for the top corners of the goal; also upper 90, for the 90-degree angle of the post and crossbar

---

Great Player Nicknames

Javier "Chicharito" Hernandez (means "Little Pea")
Lionel "The Flea" Messi
Cristiano "O Robo" Ronaldo (means "The Robot")
Zlatan "Ibra" Ibrahimovic

GLOSSARY

assists (uh-SISTS) passes from one teammate to another that lead directly to a goal

dribbling (DRIB-ul-ing) moving a soccer ball by using small taps and touches of the feet

forehead (FORE-hed) the part of a human face above the eyebrows and below the hairline

foul (FOWL) an action that is against the rules of a sport

graceful (GRAYCE-full) able to move smoothly and easily without clumsiness

hexagons (HEX-uh-gahnz) shapes with six equal sides

pentagons (PENT-uh-gahnz) shapes with five equal sides

FIND OUT MORE

IN THE LIBRARY

Hornby, Hugh. *Eyewitness: Soccer*.
New York, NY: DK Publishing, 2019.

Jökulsson, Illugi. *The World's Greatest Clubs*.
New York, NY: Abbeville Kids, 2019.

Rediger, Pat. *Soccer: For the Love of Sports*.
Calgary, AB: Weigl/AV2, 2019.

ON THE WEB

Visit our Web site for links about soccer:
childsworld.com/links

Note to Parents, Teachers, and Librarians: We routinely verify our Web links to make sure they are safe and active sites. So encourage your readers to check them out!

INDEX

Brazil, 5
defending, 12, 13
dribbling, 8, 10
FIFA, 5
field diagram, 9
futsal, 8
gear, 6, 7
goalies, 7, 8, 13, 15
Hamm, Mia, 4
heading, 12
Hernandez, Javier "Chicarito," 21
history, 4
Ibrahimovic, Zlatan "Ibra," 21
indoor soccer, 8
Messi, Lionel "The Flea," 4, 6, 21

MLS, 5
name of game, 4, 18
NWSL, 5
passing, 11
Pelé, 4, 5
positions, 17
Pugh, Mallory, 14
Rapinoe, Megan, 14
referee, 16, 18
Ronaldo, Cristiano "O Robo," 4, 14, 21
shooting, 11, 14, 20
slang, 18, 19, 20, 21
statistics, 14, 15
UEFA, 5

About the Author and Illustrator

James Buckley Jr. is the author of more than 50 books on sports for young readers, as well as many sports biographies. He lives in Santa Barbara, California. James Horvath is an illustrator and cartoonist based in California. He has written and illustrated several children's books, including Dig, Dogs, Dig! and Build, Dogs, Build!